THIS BOOK BELONGS TO

_____

AND IS A GIFT FROM

_____

I Belong

MY BAPTISM SCRAPBOOK

Introduction by Sarah Horton
Scrapbook by Valerie Gittings

Copyright © 2000 by Morehouse Publishing

Morehouse Publishing, 4775 Linglestown Road, Harrisburg, PA 17112

Morehouse Publishing, 445 Fifth Avenue, New York, NY 10016

Morehouse Publishing is an imprint of Church Publishing Incorporated.

Portions of the service of Holy Baptism reproduced herein are from
The Book of Common Prayer (1979) of the Episcopal Church, USA.

Printed in Malaysia.

Cover and page design by Trude Brummer

ISBN 978-0-8192-1849-0

Fourth Printing, 2008

I

Holy Baptism: An Introduction for Children

BY SARAH HORTON

This is a book about an important day that you may not remember. It is about the day of your baptism. This was the day your parents and godparents gave thanks in the church for God's love for you, by asking God to make you a member of the Christian Church.

You are a member of many groups in this life, and you belong in many ways. You belong in your family. You belong in your school and with your friends. You belong in clubs or groups you have joined, like Cub Scouts or Brownies. You belong in the country where you were born or where your family has come to live. And you belong to God. This is one of the most important ways you belong in the world.

The day you were baptized was not when you first started to belong to God. From the very beginning of your life God has loved you and cared about you and named you with your name. God has loved you, from the beginning, for just who you are. God will go on loving you all your life, no matter where you go or what adventures you have along the way.

You have always been loved by God. But when you were baptized something new and wonderful happened. Your godparents and your parents, or maybe one of your parents, brought you to church as a way of thanking God for loving you so much. They said "yes" to God's care of you. They said that they wanted to try to follow the way of Jesus, and that they wanted you to learn the way of Jesus as you grew up.

Because your parents and godparents said "yes" to God on your behalf, we believe that you have now become God's child in a whole new way. That way has to do with the life and death of Jesus, who showed us what God is like.

Jesus lived and died for us. He was resurrected to new life so that we could always know that God is for us. That new life is given to us in the presence of the Risen Christ through God's Holy Spirit. When you were baptized you, too, became part of God's new life.

In your life as a baptized Christian, others will help you learn that Jesus loves and cares for all of us and forgives our sins. Jesus also helps us to work with God for the well-being of the whole creation—not only God's people but animals and the whole natural world that God created.

The people of the Church all are part of this new life, and so when you were baptized you became a member of the Church. You joined in with all the countless men and women and children who give thanks to God and try faithfully to be God's people.

On the day of your baptism your godparents and parents made promises for you, saying that they would help you understand these promises as you grew up. These promises are part of what we call the Baptismal Covenant. Because God loves us and cares for us, we promise to love and care for other people, and all other living beings also.

In the Baptismal Covenant we say that we will try to understand that each person is loved by God and that each person is worthy of God's love. We say that we will try to help God make the world a better place. We will treat all people with dignity, fairness, and respect. We will try to do whatever we can to help God make the world peaceful and safe for everyone. But we know that even though we mostly try to do our best, oftentimes we mess up. We are sometimes unkind to people and hurt their feelings, just as they hurt us. In the Baptismal Covenant we say that we will always try to remember that God does forgive us when we do wrong and are sorry about it and that God helps us to make a new start.

We say also in the Baptismal Covenant that we know we can follow the way of peace and justice and love that Jesus taught us only if we ask God to help us. Part of what that means is that it is important to come to church to join with other people who are also trying to follow the way Jesus taught us.

You have most likely forgotten, though you may remember, that after these promises in the church service, water was blessed and then poured on your head by the minister. The water might have come from the font in the church. Or maybe you were immersed in a stream or pond outdoors or baptized in a special pool inside the church. Water is a very important part of the baptism. One of the reasons that water is so important is that Jesus was baptized with water by John the Baptist, as the Gospel tells us.

When Jesus was baptized with water, the Gospel says that Jesus heard from God some special words: "You are . . . the Beloved."

God means these words for each of us, also. When we are baptized our names are spoken. This helps us to remember that, right from the beginning of our lives, we are named as the beloved, each with our own particular name. We are always loved by God just for who we are.

When you were baptized your family might have been there to help you celebrate. But it is important to remember that the members of the church were there also, to give thanks for you. And in the service they said that they would help you along in your life of faith. In a special prayer after the baptism, the minister spoke for all their hopes. And this is part of what he or she prayed. The minister prayed that God would give you:

- An inquiring and discerning [that is, a wise] heart
- The courage to will and to persevere
- A spirit to know and love God
- And the gift of joy and wonder in all God's works

In all the adventures of your life

may these blessings be yours,

through the power of God's Holy Spirit.

I have always belonged to God. And on _____ ,

(date)

when I was _____ , I was baptized at _____

(age)   (name of church)

in _____

(name of town)

so that I could belong to God's church.

[INSERT PHOTO OF CHURCH]

At church, it was the season of _____.

I was wearing _____.

[INSERT PHOTO OF BABY
DRESSED FOR BAPTISM]

The family I belong to was very happy I was being baptized. My family promised to teach me how to follow the way of Jesus.

[INSERT PHOTO OF FAMILY]

"I present

_____

(baby's name)

to receive the Sacrament of Baptism."

Special wishes from my family for me on my Baptism day were

_____

_____

_____

_____

_____

_____

My godparents were _____

_____.

They promised, along with my family, to be sure that I would be taught the things I need to know so that I can belong to God's church my whole life.

[INSERT PHOTO OF BABY
WITH GODPARENTS]

"Will you be responsible for seeing that the child you present is brought up in the Christian faith and life?"

"I will, with God's help."

Special wishes from my godparents for me on my Baptism day were

_____

_____

_____

_____

_____

Other relatives and friends who took part in my Baptism were _____

_____

_____

_____

[INSERT PHOTO OF BAPTISMAL

PARTY AND GUESTS]

All the other people who belong to the Church said they would help me to belong too.

[INSERT PHOTO OF CONGREGATION]

"Will you who witness these vows
do all in your power to support
these persons in their life in Christ?"

Special wishes from my relatives and friends for me on my Baptism day were

_____

_____

_____

_____

_____

_____

The priest who performed my Baptism, _____,

poured water on my forehead and said words that meant that, even as a little baby,

I had a place in the church and that I always would.

[INSERT PHOTO OF PRIEST]

"I baptize you in the name
of the Father, and of the Son,
and of the Holy Spirit."

The priest's special wishes for me on the day of my Baptism were _____

_____

_____

_____

_____

_____

A special Scripture said at my Baptism was _____

_____

_____

_____

_____

_____

A special prayer said for me at my Baptism was _____

_____

_____

_____

_____

_____

After my Baptism, we all went to_____

_____.

[INSERT PHOTO OF PARTY]

"You are sealed by the Holy Spirit

in Baptism and marked as

Christ's own forever."

Some of the gifts I received on my Baptism day were _____

_____

_____

_____

_____

_____

Holy Baptism

Presentation and Examination of the Candidates

The Celebrant says

The Candidate(s) for Holy Baptism will now be presented.

Adults and Older Children

The candidates who are able to answer for themselves are presented individually by their Sponsors, as follows

Sponsor   I present N. to receive the Sacrament of Baptism.

The Celebrant asks each candidate when presented

Do you desire to be baptized?

Candidate I do.

Infants and Younger Children

Then the candidates unable to answer for themselves are presented individually by their Parents and Godparents, as follows

Parents and Godparents
I present N. to receive the Sacrament of Baptism.

When all have been presented the Celebrant asks the parents and godparents

Will you be responsible for seeing that the child you present
is brought up in the Christian faith and life?

Parents and Godparents
I will, with God's help.

Celebrant

Will you by your prayers and witness help this child to grow
into the full stature of Christ?

Parents and Godparents
I will, with God's help.

*Then the Celebrant asks the following questions of the candidates who
can speak for themselves, and of the parents and godparents who speak
on behalf of the infants and younger children*

Question Do you renounce Satan and all the spiritual forces
of wickedness that rebel against God?
Answer I renounce them.

Question Do you renounce the evil powers of this world
which corrupt and destroy the creatures of God?
Answer I renounce them.

Question	Do you renounce all sinful desires that draw you from the love of God?
Answer	I renounce them.
Question	Do you turn to Jesus Christ and accept him as your Savior?
Answer	I do.
Question	Do you put your whole trust in his grace and love?
Answer	I do.
Question	Do you promise to follow and obey him as your Lord?
Answer	I do.

After all have been presented, the Celebrant addresses the congregation, saying

Will you who witness these vows do all in your
power to support these persons in their life in Christ?

People	We will.

The Celebrant then says these or similar words

Let us join with those who are committing themselves to Christ
and renew our own baptismal covenant.

The Baptismal Covenant

Celebrant	Do you believe in God the Father?
People	I believe in God, the Father almighty, creator of heaven and earth.

Celebrant	Do you believe in Jesus Christ, the Son of God?
People	I believe in Jesus Christ, his only Son, our Lord.

        He was conceived by the power of the Holy Spirit
          and born of the Virgin Mary.
        He suffered under Pontius Pilate,
          was crucified, died, and was buried.
        He descended to the dead.
        On the third day he rose again.
        He ascended into heaven,
          and is seated at the right hand of the Father.
        He will come again to judge the living and the dead.

Celebrant	Do you believe in God the Holy Spirit?
People	I believe in the Holy Spirit,

        the holy catholic Church,
        the communion of saints,
        the forgiveness of sins,
        the resurrection of the body,
        and the life everlasting.

Celebrant	Will you continue in the apostles' teaching and fellowship, in the breaking of bread, and in the prayers?
People	I will, with God's help.
Celebrant	Will you persevere in resisting evil, and, whenever you fall into sin, repent and return to the Lord?

People	I will, with God's help.
Celebrant	Will you proclaim by word and example the Good News of God in Christ?
People	I will, with God's help.
Celebrant	Will you seek and serve Christ in all persons, loving your neighbor as yourself?
People	I will, with God's help.
Celebrant	Will you strive for justice and peace among all people, and respect the dignity of every human being?
People	I will, with God's help.

Prayers for the Candidates

The Celebrant then says to the congregation

Let us now pray for these persons who are to receive the Sacrament of new birth [and for those (this person) who have renewed their commitment to Christ.]

A Person appointed leads the following petitions

Leader	Deliver them, O Lord, from the way of sin and death.
People	Lord, hear our prayer.

| Leader | Open their hearts to your grace and truth. |
| People | Lord, hear our prayer. |

| Leader | Fill them with your holy and life-giving Spirit. |
| People | Lord, hear our prayer. |

| Leader | Keep them in the faith and communion of your holy Church. |
| People | Lord, hear our prayer. |

| Leader | Teach them to love others in the power of the Spirit. |
| People | Lord, hear our prayer. |

| Leader | Send them into the world in witness to your love. |
| People | Lord, hear our prayer. |

| Leader | Bring them to the fullness of your peace and glory. |
| People | Lord, hear our prayer. |

The Celebrant says

Grant, O Lord, that all who are baptized into the death
of Jesus Christ your Son may live in the power of his
resurrection and look for him to come again in glory; who
lives and reigns now and for ever. *Amen.*

Thanksgiving over the Water

The Celebrant blesses the water, first saying

The Lord be with you.

| People | And also with you. |

Celebrant	Let us give thanks to the Lord our God.
People	It is right to give him thanks and praise.
Celebrant	We thank you, Almighty God, for the gift of water. Over it the Holy Spirit moved in the beginning of creation. Through it you led the children of Israel out of their bondage in Egypt into the land of promise. In it your Son Jesus received the baptism of John and was anointed by the Holy Spirit as the Messiah, the Christ, to lead us, through his death and resurrection, from the bondage of sin into everlasting life.

We thank you, Father, for the water of Baptism. In it we are buried with Christ in his death. By it we share in his resurrection. Through it we are reborn by the Holy Spirit. Therefore in joyful obedience to your Son, we bring into his fellowship those who come to him in faith, baptizing them in the Name of the Father, and of the Son, and of the Holy Spirit.

At the following words, the Celebrant touches the water

Now sanctify this water, we pray you, by the power of your Holy Spirit, that those who here are cleansed from sin and born again may continue for ever in the risen life of Jesus Christ our Savior.

To him, to you, and to the Holy Spirit, be all honor and glory, now and for ever. *Amen.*

Consecration of the Chrism

The Bishop may then consecrate oil of Chrism, placing a hand on the vessel of oil, and saying

Eternal Father, whose blessed Son was anointed by the
Holy Spirit to be the Savior and servant of all, we pray you to
consecrate this oil, that those who are sealed with it may
share in the royal priesthood of Jesus Christ; who lives and
reigns with you and the Holy Spirit, for ever and ever. *Amen.*

The Baptism

Each candidate is presented by name to the Celebrant, or to an assisting priest or deacon, who then immerses, or pours water upon, the candidate, saying

N., I baptize you in the Name of the Father, and of the Son,
and of the Holy Spirit. *Amen.*

When this action has been completed for all candidates, the Bishop or Priest, at a place in full sight of the congregation, prays over them, saying

Let us pray.

Heavenly Father, we thank you that by water and the Holy
Spirit you have bestowed upon these your servants the
forgiveness of sin, and have raised them to the new life of

grace. Sustain them, O Lord, in your Holy Spirit. Give them an inquiring and discerning heart, the courage to will and to persevere, a spirit to know and to love you, and the gift of joy and wonder in all your works. *Amen.*

Then the Bishop or Priest places a hand on the person's head, marking on the forehead the sign of the cross [using Chrism if desired] and saying to each one

N., you are sealed by the Holy Spirit in Baptism and marked as Christ's own for ever. *Amen.*

Or this action may be done immediately after the administration of the water and before the preceding prayer.
When all have been baptized, the Celebrant says
> Let us welcome the newly baptized.

Celebrant and People
> We receive you into the household of God. Confess the faith of Christ crucified, proclaim his resurrection, and share with us in his eternal priesthood.

If Confirmation, Reception, or the Reaffirmation of Baptismal Vows is not to follow, the Peace is now exchanged

Celebrant The peace of the Lord be always with you.
People And also with you.

CPSIA information can be obtained
at www.ICGtesting.com
Printed in the USA
LVHW020056050919
629805LV00001B/3/P